Figure Drawing Workbook

Rhythm and Language of the Human Form,
Volume 2

Gabrielle Dahms

Booksmart Press LLC

Book Cover by 100Covers

Images by the author and Pixabay.

Published by Booksmart Press LLC

ISBN 13: 979-8-9853675-4-6 (paperback)

ISBN 13: 979-8-9853675-5-3 (ebook)

Publisher's Cataloging-in-Publication Data

Names:Dahms, Gabrielle, author.

Title:Figure drawing workbook: rhythm and language of the human form / Gabrielle Dahms.

Description:Includes bibliographical references and index. | Cheyenne, WY: Booksmart Press,2024.

Identifiers:LCCN: 2024919961 | ISBN: 979-8-9853675-4-6 (paperback) | 979-8-9853675-5-3(ebook)
Subjects: LCSH Human figure in art--Problems, exercises, etc. |Drawing--Technique. | BISAC ART/ Subjects & Themes / Human Figure | ART/Techniques / Drawing | ART/ Techniques / Life Drawing | ART / Subjects& Themes / Portraits | ART/ Techniques / Composition
Classification: LCC NC765 .D34 2024 | DDC 743/.4--dc23

Dedication

To all outstanding teachers on whose shoulders I stand.
With special acknowledgement to Sharon Pearson and Alan Mc-Corkle.

Contents

Introduction

IF YOU ENJOYED *FIGURE Drawing: Rhythm and Language of the Human Form Vol. I,* you now hold the book's accompanying workbook. Used consistently, the exercises in it will propel your artistic skills forward.

The exercises address many of the fundamentals you need to excel in to represent the human figure on a two-dimensional page, realistically, expressively, and imbued with your own artistic vision.

They concern themselves with the many aspects discussed in *Volume 1.* Some are timed, others are not. Spend at least three to five hours a week on developing your drawing skills, or more if you can.

Reading books about drawing the human figure cannot and will not replace consistent and continual practice.

The drawing exercises develop the perceptual, technical, and expressive skills and syntax that lend life, beauty and communicative tenets to your drawings.

One additional consideration is this one: before drawing anything, walk around the model or object. See them from different angles and different vantage points, then find what interests you. See that in your mind's eye.

Then use your drawing arm and hand and start drawing the model in the air. You will have drawn the major centers and gestures before you ever commit them to paper. Doing so creates a memory of the pose in your body. Over time, your body memory will serve you well when drawing, though it is important to note that you must learn to trust it.

The first marks you make on your paper are gestural marks. Drawing ability and gesture intimately relate.

Draw the figure as though it were transparent. Capturing the pose's essence is almost as though there is nothing there. You are drawing energy, not the figure. When you get a feeling for the pose, for your paper and the marks you make, that feeling allows you to drive right through the pose. The figure appears because of drawing its energy.

I know this sounds like magic, but it isn't.

To capture the complete pose and its attitude, start at the feet—from feet to head—using simple and economical marks. Account for the waist and the tilt of the hips. The energy of the pose springs up out of the floor!

Draw in layers. Extract the gesture and get excited about the action of the pose. Always fortify the action as expressed through its gesture with structure.

Develop x-ray vision and look into the form, into the pose. Move through the form from large to small. Drawing is like life, requires you to start in the center of things to "get it." Your drawing tool, whether charcoal, pencil, brush or pen, connects to what your eye sees. In fact, you are internalizing what you are about to draw into your hand, meaning that your hand is as much a drawing tool as that which touches your paper and records the marks and lines.

When you see two forms, find out how they relate to one another. Remember that nothing is ever separate. Look at the overlap of forms and also at negative shapes. When moving from one form to another, stay connected always. Every form has its own center, energy, and expression.

The best part of the gesture, the action of the pose, is doing it again and again. It reveals the beauty of something alive. Everything in the body is doing something that is about to move. And everything has a gesture: the head, the nose, the eyes, the hair, the neck, and on and on it goes.

Gestural drawing is your investigation of the pose, no matter how long the pose. Your knowledge of the structure that underlies the figure and the pose allows you to show what is happening in front of you on your two-dimensional paper. All true innovation and invention depends on gestural expression and structural knowledge—yes, on anatomy and myology. You meld art and science in your work, and your artistic expression arises from this.

If you think that's a lot of work, you are right, but it is so worth it. While intellectually understanding this offers much value, producing art requires constant, regular application. No substitute exists for practice.

The exercises this workbook contains offer practice starting points for you, always ready to use excellent reference materials. I provide you with them in the book this Workbook complements.

Commit to five to seven hours of drawing practice a week. That may sound minimal for an endeavor which demands thousands of hours to excel in it. If you wish to become a master, enjoy this process and set it in motion today.

The secret of getting ahead is getting started.

Mark Twain

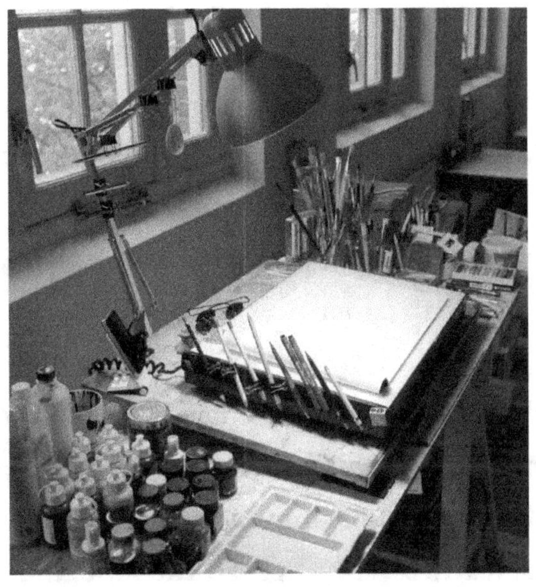

Chapter One

Drawing Exercises

You are on the right track in your quest to become a skilled artist. Only regular, repeated practice brings you closer and closer to that aim. Practice, combined with careful study of the model, the environment, movement, and easy access to several excellent reference books, is tantamount. No other panacea exists.

Repeat all the exercises in the following sections multiple times. In fact, that is the only way to master them.

Enjoy the process and every improvement, no matter how small!

<u>Instructions for Drawing Exercises</u>

The following applies to all drawing exercises in this booklet. Allocate 30 to 45 minutes to start. Detailed structural drawings will take longer than this.

Also experiment with varying paper size and scale in these drawings. Work with paper sizes 10x14 or larger, but no larger than 18x24.

In all your drawings, avoid too much detail and focus on simplified forms. For example, when drawing the head and face, the planes of the head and simple shading must be there before drawing the features, such as eyes, the nose, the mouth, etc.

In all drawing exercises, remember that the body comprises many layers and that ALL of them interact with one another.

Everything is dependent upon everything else.

Sharon Pearson

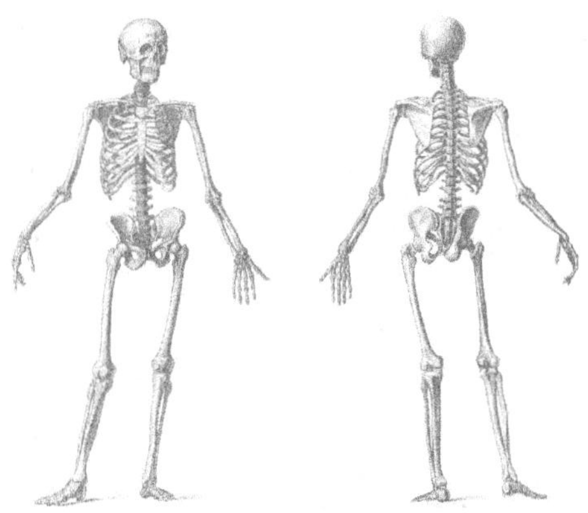

Chapter Two

Anatomy
Building Foundational Skills

THESE DRAWING EXERCISES PROVIDE you with insight into what lies under a figure's skin. They enable you to penetrate unseen forms that shape what the skin holds.

1. Your first exercise involves NO drawing, just looking and seeing: visually parse the model and identify the body's skeletal/anatomical forms. Those are the forms which underlie the model's (or any person's body). Mentally identify the positions of the anatomical forms

and how they relate to one another. Do this for 3 to 5 minutes and keep in mind never to stare down the model.

Part 2 of this exercise is for you to draw as much of what you saw from memory. Pay special attention to capturing the major anatomical masses.

2. In your mind's eye, behold the mechanics that follow the structures you discerned in exercise no. 1. Now draw the figure again with the mechanics in mind.

3. Now draw gestural and simple representations of the forms you learned about in no. 1 and no. 2.

4. Get a model of the human skeleton and draw it.
Small skeleton models are available in art supply stores or online. While valuable tools, the smaller the skeleton model, the less detail it contains. For more exact anatomy drawings, either use a life-size skeleton or opt to copy anatomy drawings by the masters.

Or draw the life size skeleton that often collects dust in most drawing classes.

5. Draw the human skeleton from
- The front

- The back

- The sides

- A three-quarter view

6. Draw the anatomy of different parts of the body:
  - Hands

  - Feet

  - Heads

  - The rib cage

  - The legs

  - The arms

  - And the many other bones comprising the human body.

7. Abstract the various forms and shapes of the body and the pose by drawing their corresponding geometrical shapes.

8. Refer to anatomical drawings by Leonardo DaVinci and Michaelangelo, for example, or select from photographs of the skeleton. Find them online or in an art book or in a museum. Copy them.

9. Find an illustration that interests you in your spiffy anatomy book. You have one, right?
If not, get a good anatomy reference book right away.
Copy the illustration of the anatomical structure you choose with

- Graphite

- Pencil

- Colored pencils

- Charcoal

- Watercolor

- Pen and ink

10. Abstract the forms of the skeleton by drawing their masses in geometric shapes.

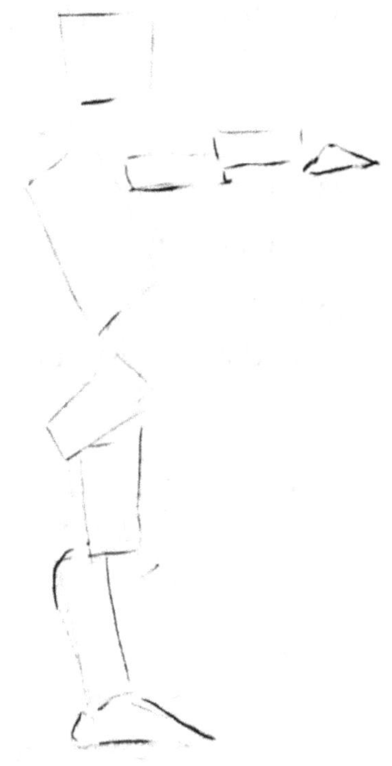

Chapter Three

Masses, Centers, Volume, and Weight

Delineating Forms and Rhythms of the Body

MASSES, CENTERS, VOLUME, AND weight afford the figure balance and grace. All bodies have forms that counteract and complement one another.

1. As you observe the model and the pose, draw abstract geometrical forms for the masses and limbs of the body. Account for masses and limbs you may not see because of the pose. Doing so balances the figure and the composition. Find out how the forms relate to one another.

2. Study and draw abstract forms, such as cylinders, ovals, and cubes. Find out how they move in space and how perspective affects them.

3. Draw the same pose from various angles. Move around to do so, but always consider others when you do this.

4. Ask a clothed friend, relative or acquaintance to pose for you and draw the draped fabric. Drapery folds hold light and shadow and rely on the form underlying it.

5. Set up a still life with draped fabric. No model necessary.

6. Study and draw abstract forms, such as cylinders, ovals, and cubes, give them a ground and shade them according to the light source on them.

7. Compose a still life with apples or oranges or peppers or all of them. Light your still life with a single light source, a spotlight.

Observe the difference the light source makes in various positions and angles.

8. Compose a drawing study of a single fruit or vegetable. You choose which one.

Experiment with different media and papers. Shade the forms to capture volume and form.

9. Draw a draped male figure.

10. Draw a draped female figure.
For exercises no. 9 and no. 10, you may:

- *Use a life model*

- *Copy a master drawing*

- *Use a photograph*

Take your time as you also assess the media you use. Use easily erasable media in all of your first drawings. Graduate to other media as your skills and confidence grow.

11. Go back to abstract geometrical forms which for the pose, and shade in the areas carrying the body's weight.

Notice where the weight appears in a standing pose. Unless the model stands in a frontal, completely aligned, and static position in front of you, the weight is likely to be on one leg.

You can test this out by doing a quick assessment when standing by bending or turning to one side. Which leg carries the weight to support your body in these positions?

When you draw the model, see how he or she carries the body's weight. Simple initial shading, being darker in weight-bearing limbs, shows the weight.

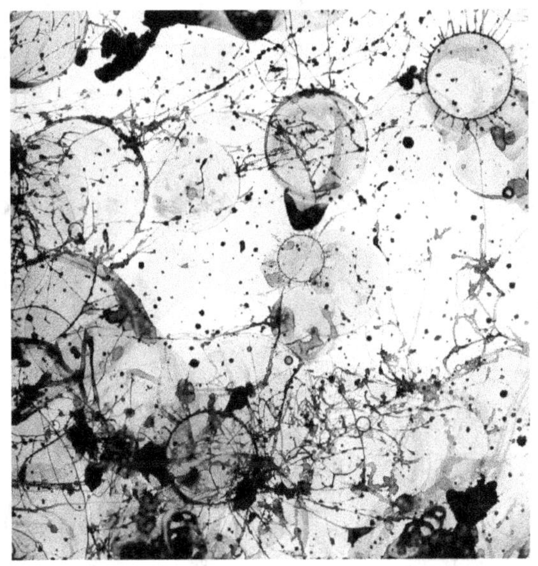

Chapter Four

Composition Drawing

Taking Composition to the Next Level

COMPOSITION REFERS TO THE most effective placement of the figure in its surroundings. While many ways to compose a drawing exist, lending it a particular focal point or focal points, aim for simplicity and balance when you learn the craft.

1. Take your viewer and hold it in front of you so you can see the object you wish to draw. I usually close one eye to better direct what I am seeing, but you may wish to experiment and find what works for you.

Focus on how you want to balance the figure, its grounding, and any other elements on the paper.

Practice this over and over with different figures and objects.

2. Draw a few smaller frames onto your paper. Newsprint suffices. Fit thumbnail sketches of the drawing object into these frames, employing different angles and perspectives.

3. Take your viewfinder and move it to various positions when looking at the model. Remember to hold it at arm's length.

Perhaps move around the model (from a distance) with your viewfinder.

Record several compositions you just saw on your paper. Quick sketches are fine. This is about all elements in a composition and how they fit the page.

Find some interesting perspectives while doing so.

4. Look at photographs of people and see which compositions compel you and why. Take notes as you complete the process.

5. Compositions are about balancing the visual elements in a drawing.

Go to a museum and look at drawings and paintings of people and portraits.

Take notes about what you observe as it relates to composition. What works? What does not? Where does your eye travel?

6. Study the drawings and paintings of Michaelangelo, Rembrandt, Ingres, Degas, Picasso, and Matisse for a compositional understanding of their works.

These artists are a few of the many examples of masters you can study for this purpose. Find others.

Take notes.

7. Draw a composition as one of the masters would have. You are not copying their work, though that is valuable as well.

For this exercise, your aim is to apply compositional principles as the masters did.

Repeat this drawing exercise for all artists who interest you.

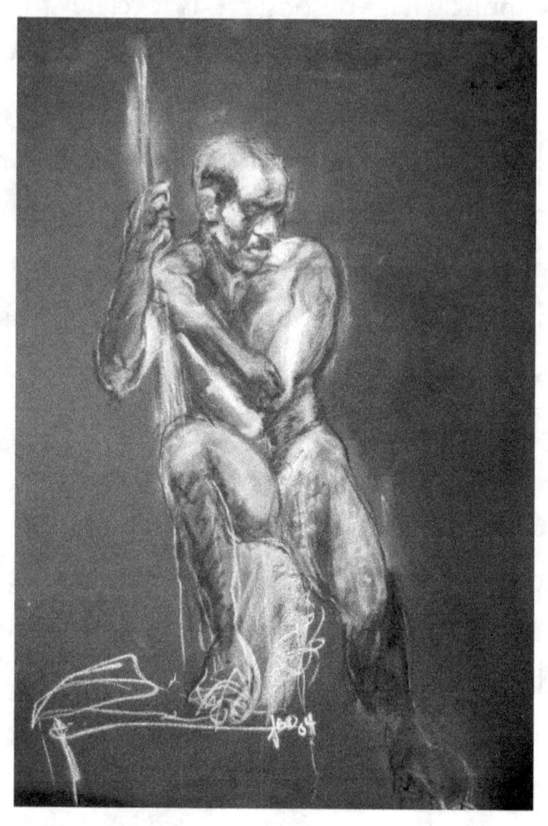

Chapter Five

Negative Space

Learning to See What's In Between and Around the Figure

NEGATIVE SPACE DEFINES FORMS on the inside and outside of the figure. Among its many purposes, the creation of a sense of space and of visual clarity also lends the figure focus.

1. Use your viewer to frame the figure you want to draw. Squint your eye to achieve better focus when doing so. Start by drawing the negative space versus focusing on the figure. The figure arises from the negative space.

2. Shade your entire paper surface with a charcoal grounding, then use your erasers to draw the space surrounding the figure, as well as the negative spaces within the figure, say the space between the arm and the torso when they do not touch.

3. With any person or object, draw around it and fill the surrounding space with your medium of choice. For this exercise, charcoal is great.

The shape of the person or object will be the color of your paper.

This differs from a line drawing because it creates the form of the model or other objects you are drawing by filling the negative space around it.

Make negative space studies and drawings of:

- A plant

- A seated person

- A cup

- Oranges, apples or other fruits

- Cars

- Chairs

4. Do a self-portrait by filling in the negative space around your head.

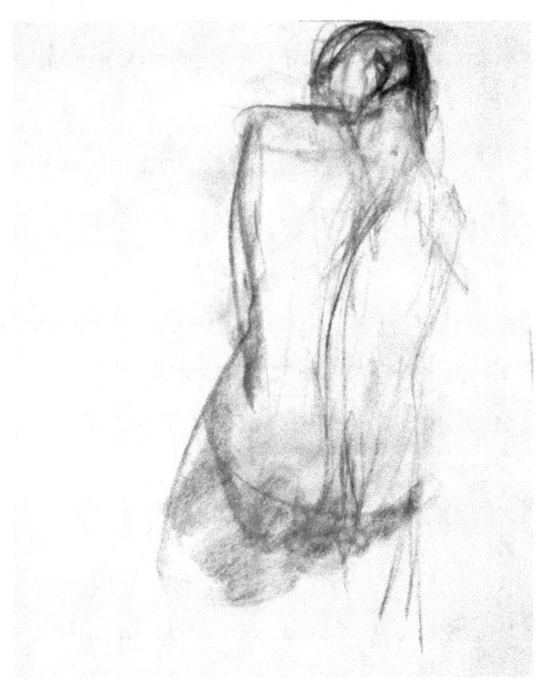

Chapter Six

Gesture, Rhythm and Movement Drawing Exercises

Pursuing Dynamism and Beauty

Gesture, rhythm, and movement intrinsically connect. They underlie all drawings, whether of the figure or anything else.

1. The park, the symphony, the ballet, and many, many other public spaces are wonderful venues for gestural drawings. Choose one of them, your sketchbook and pencil or ink pen at the ready, find a space to sit or stand and draw. First observe your surroundings for a few minutes, then draw simple representations of persons walking by or twisting, turning, or bending.

2. Draw at least thirty to forty quick gestures of no longer than 30-seconds each. You are likely to find that you must draw quickly to capture the poses because your "models" here are not posing for you.

3. Make a gestural line drawing of a person, people, or the class model.

4. Continue one or more of the no. 3 drawings with a sustained gesture.

Sustained gesture drawings rely on a quick gestural drawing as their basis, then continuing with gestural marks that develop the drawing on top of and besides the initial gestural marks you capture.

5. Take an 18x24 sheet of paper and divide it to fit some 15 action poses. Now start drawing the poses the model presents you. Poses that last 10, 20, 30 seconds and no longer than a minute are best for this exercise.

6. Take an 18x24 sheet of paper and divide it to fit some 15 resting poses. Now start drawing the poses the model presents you. Poses that last 10, 20, 30 seconds and no longer than a minute are best for this exercise.

7. Draw the energetic flow of the body's rhythm in simple lines without details and with economy.

8. Draw the human figure in abstract forms, such as cylinders, ovals, and cubes. Then find the tension lines that connect these forms.

9. Abstract the figure by drawing gestural lines and assess their weight, tension, and rhythm. Observe how these economical and simple marks communicate attitudes and emotions.

10. Draw a pose with the dynamics of movement in it.

For example, a runner at the ready to start a sprint. Even though we think about that position as stationary and non-moving, the tensed muscles are ready to spring into action. You can feel the movement, although it has not yet happened. Focus on the gesture only.

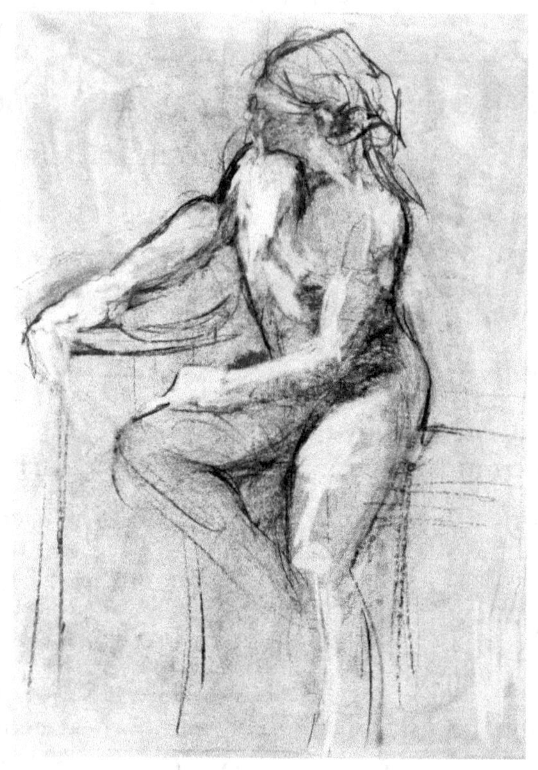

Chapter Seven

Light and Shadow

Adding Volume and Depth

THE THREE-DIMENSIONAL HUMAN FORM comes to life with light and shadow, even if they alone never make a drawing by themselves.

1. Draw a cylinder or a cube in perspective with a light source in place, generally a spot light. Using two values, shade in the form.

2. Look at the model in the arranged lighting set-up and note the light and shadow defining the body's forms. Now draw the figure with values only.

3. Draw the planes of

- The head

- The hand

- The foot

- The torso

- The pelvis

- The rib cage

Modeling them with light and shade, creating values, only. You may use a kneaded eraser to help you model the forms. Kneaded erasers are drawing tools.

4. Use a soft charcoal stick and cover your entire drawing page with a charcoal ground. Then use your kneaded eraser to model the model's form on the page.

5. In this drawing exercise, break the body's forms down into their geometrical equivalents. Think of boxes, spheres, cubes, and cylinders. Shade each of these forms to create depth.

You can also draw these forms individually, then shade them. You draw a box, for example, and shade it.

6. Set up a still life with a geometric form, such as a ball or an orange, or a box or a house, etc. and light it with a spot light. Then draw the object, shade it and draw its cast shadow.

7. Vary exercise no. 3 by moving the light source to a different place that still allows it to light the object. Then draw as instructed in exercise no. 3.

Notice the shadows and reflected light that arises from lighting the model with a spotlight. The way the figure in front of you (or anything for that matter) is lit, makes an enormous difference in what you see and how you see the figure. This naturally translates to any drawing you render.

8. Take out 5 to 10 photographs and determine where the light is coming from and how it affects the images. How can you tell?

   1. Make a drawing in which you shade the form, either the figure or another object, such as a piece of fruit. Use pencil for this drawing and shade the forms using a full value range.

2. Now draw and shade the same pose or still life in colored pencil, again using a full value range. Notice how using color affects the values and thereby the shading.

3. Repeat this exercise with charcoal, with watercolor, or pen and ink. Notice how the shading and the values it creates differ in these media.

4. Compare all the drawings you produced in this exercise to appreciate how the shading creates depth in these drawings. How are they similar or different?

Note: You may also copy a photograph in this way. If you do, observe how the drawing might differ from a life model or a still life object with a light source on it.

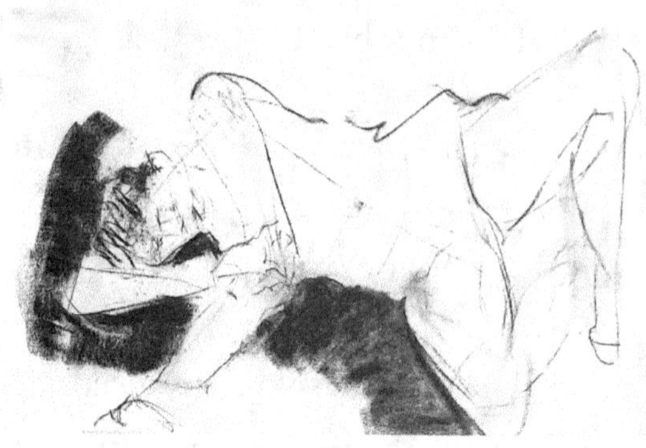

Chapter Eight

Planes and Perspective

Creating Depth

PLANES AND PERSPECTIVES HELP discern the three-dimensional forms of the human body. These forms and perspectives change, depending on the position of the body and its parts and from where the viewer observes the figure. Learning to simplify them by applying imaginary lines helps capture the forms.

1. In a medium of your choice, draw outlines of geometric forms onto the page without shading them. Cover your page with them. Next, erase a few of them and draw them again, now overlapping

some others on the page. Add a horizon line to the drawing. Observe how the forms appear to move through space with these steps.

2. Use the drawing you created in the first exercise and color it, remembering that the objects that are closest to the viewer are in sharper focus and more defined than the ones farther away. You can create this illusion by shading or coloring the closest objects darker than the ones that appear to recede in space.

3. If you have a model, draw the same pose in these perspectives:

- From below. You are most likely seated for this.

- From the front.

- From the side.

- From above. This only works if you are in a higher position relative to the model.

4. Divide your page by drawing a horizontal line across it at approximately a third its height. Choose a point on the horizontal line. The horizontal line equates to eye level. Any point on that line will do, though it is easiest to focus on one approaching the mid-point of the horizontal line.

Next, draw lines that radiate in all directions from the vanishing point you just marked on your horizontal line. Now draw some simple boxes onto the page.

Note that drawing the boxes above the horizontal line means the viewer sees these objects from below, while anything place below the horizontal line means the viewer see the objects from above.

Shade or color the boxes. As you spend time on this exercise, you might make it more fun by giving the boxes more identity. That could mean one of them turns into a house, another into a container or an old-fashioned tv set, yet another into a book and so on. Keep it simple.

Spend time on this exercise so your brain remembers the activity and grasps the concept.

Have fun!

5. Draw a cube in different perspectives under the same light source. Observe how doing so from different perspectives dramatically shifts values.

6. Draw the planes of the head.
You may shade them in to give depth and lend them readability.

7. Draw the model's pose, the entire body, as geometric forms. In this case, do so via three-dimensional boxes. Draw how these boxes relate to one another.
Shade them so plane changes become obvious.
Materials to use: A graphite pencil, preferably light, or a carbon pencil or charcoal. Finer-grained or smooth paper.

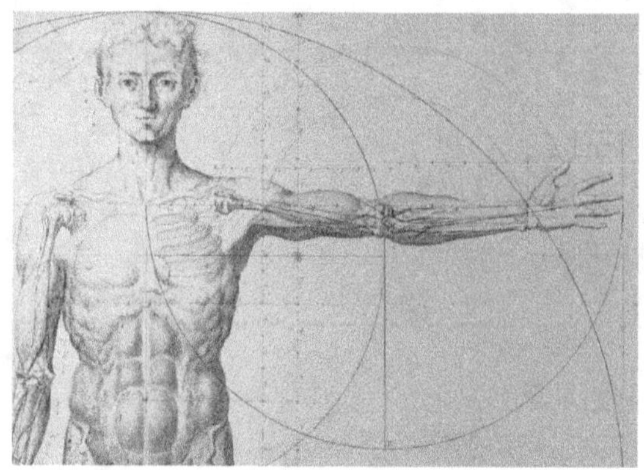

Chapter Nine

Proportions

Assessing Length and Width of Forms

THE BODY'S PROPORTIONS PROVIDE artists with references for accurate representation of the human form. Certain lengths and widths define the relationship between body parts, differing according to gender and age.

1. Draw as many stick figures in the span of an hour as you can to learn about proportions and get them right. Draw no flesh on the body's bones yet.

Make sure the head is in proportion to the rest of the body.

2. Go to a park or a public place and observe the male, female, and child bodies passing you. Note their differences. After observing for at least 15 minutes, draw what you have seen from memory.

3. Keeping in mind the conventional figure drawing measure of seven and a half heads for the human figure, draw

- A woman

- A man

- A baby

- A child

- An old person

Note the anatomical difference between them and find the waist in all of them.

4. Look at a curved surface as it appears on your model. For example, the shape of muscles in the arms and legs.

Now, abstract the curved surface with a line that preserves its direction to find its simple shape. Next, find how the shape you just identified relates to other surrounding areas and eventually to the entire body.

Identify whether the abstracted shapes are too long or too short. One easy way to do this is to use your sighting stick.

Do this exercise with different models and body types.

5. Look at some geometrical forms, such as a rectangle, a square, a circle, an ellipse, or other shapes. Some of these shapes might be irregular.

Start this exercise with the shapes as flat ones versus three-dimensional versions of them.

Once you have looked at these forms, put away your reference for them and draw them from memory.

Repeat this exercise as often as necessary until you have internalized the forms.

6. Look at the same shapes as in no. 5 above and find a reference that shows them in various positions in space: from the top, the sides, the bottom, and so on.

Study what they look like, then put away the reference sheet and draw them from memory.

Repeat this exercise as often as necessary until you have internalized the forms.

Exercises nos. 5 and 6 are fundamental in helping you get proportions right.

Your sighting stick does wonders as well.

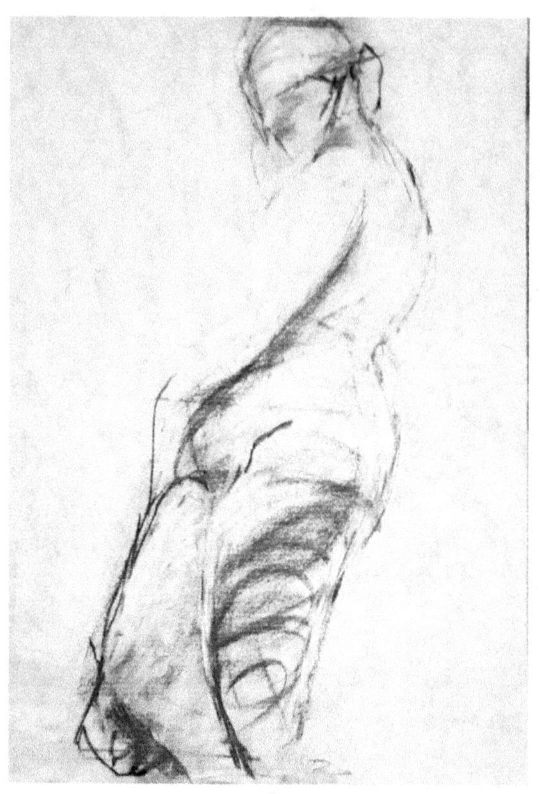

Chapter Ten

Foreshortening

Dealing with Shifting Shapes

When forms, including those of the human body, move in the space they occupy and with that closer or farther away from the viewer, these forms appear longer or shorter than they actually are. This, in turn, produces certain points of view, which often are dramatic.

1. Use a pencil or a light medium for this exercise. Draw a cylinder moving back in space, then fill its form with coils and see how the form that comes toward you is bigger than its remainder that recedes in space.

2. Using geometrical abstraction for the arms or the legs of the figure, draw as you did in exercise number 1. Note the form closest to you and the viewer is larger than other portions of the form. What you see here requires a basic understanding of anatomy to realistically and believably render the forms.

When drawing a limb, foreshortened or not, of a figure, always start at the point where the limb connects to the body, then go outward. Otherwise your drawing's proportions will be off and strange looking.

3. Draw a figure seated on the ground with the legs coming toward you. In this exercise, put down a ground plane the figure sits on. Something grid-like is best here. Observe how this grounding gives you an excellent sense about how the figure occupies space.

Again, start with abstract shapes for the legs and the feet and begin your coiled shading of the limbs at the point at which they meet the body.

4. Draw a figure leaning back, perhaps against a wall. Note and measure the parts of the body that recede and those that come towards you.

5. Draw an arm coming forward, meaning towards you, with the hand signaling *stop*.

6. Ask a friend to pose for you with his or her head bending to one side, either supported by one hand or a pillow or wall. Now draw the pose.

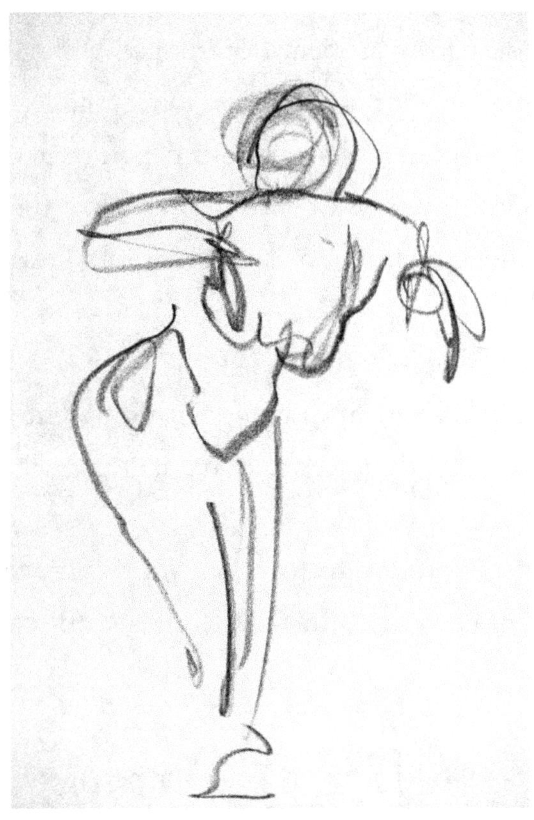

Chapter Eleven

Contour and Line

Defining Marks

LINES AND CONTOURS OFFER their own beauty in their variations. They also define forms and create depth.

1. Stand or sit with your pencil or ink pen with a starting point of your choosing on your paper. Relax your shoulders. Now look at the model and without looking at your paper, trace the contour of the figure. Continue until the contour is complete, then look at your drawing. The drawing may look strange to you. Please don't worry about that.

2. Practice blind contour drawing with different poses or with objects, your own hands or feet, and so on.

3. While blind contour informs about your ability to see, you may also draw the model's contour by looking at your paper once in a while.

4. Look at the model as the tip of your pen, pencil, or charcoal touches the paper. Then start to draw internal lines of the pose and the model, never looking at the paper.

5. For this contour and line drawing you may alter looking at the model and your paper. Notice the difference in what you see and record.

6. Draw a continuous line contour of

- Your hand.
- Your foot.

7. Draw the following with your non-dominant hand:

- A partially blind contour of the model.

- A blind contour from another vantage point.

8. Picasso was, among other things, a master at contour drawing. Find a Picasso contour drawing in a book or online. If online, print out the drawing.

In either case, turn the drawing upside down and copy it.

Afterwards, look at your copy and ascertain what you saw and what was missing.

9. Draw a hand or foot or face in cross contour lines. These are lines which travel across the form's surface. They can be straight, curved or spherical and that depends on the surface form.

10. Put two dots on your paper, then connect the dots with a crisp line. It is freehand drawing, but you can do it. If it looks wobbly at first, keep practicing.

Remember your own body mechanics as you draw.

Fill the page with as many straight, crisp lines as will fit, drawing the lines down and up, angled, right to left, and left to right.

Do this as fast as possible.

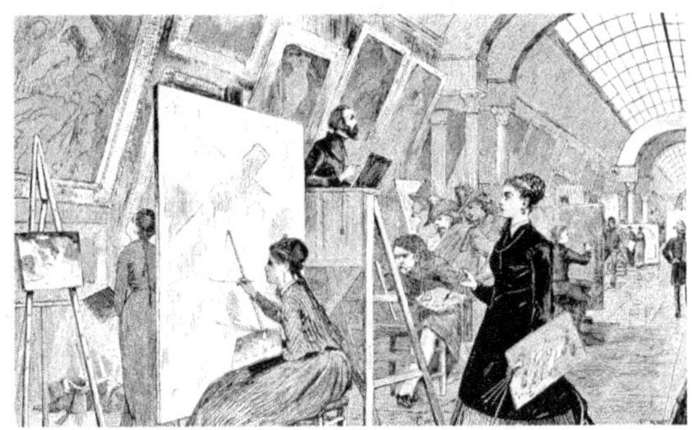

Chapter Twelve

Museum Drawing
Taking Your Drawing Public

KEEPING YOUR FOCUS IN a museum's gallery can be a challenging because museums are busy. The surrounding bustle offers distractions and because museum goers stand close to or right in front of works of art, it might be difficult to capture what you want. That means you are developing your ability to sketch and draw under pressure and as quickly as possible.

1. Walk around a gallery for inspiration before you settle in front of a piece. Once in front of it, take some notes about its composition, colors, mood, technique, abstraction, and so forth.

Find a spot that is farther away than normal and sketch the work from that vantage point. You will not see all the details.

2. Stay with the work you found in no. 1, but now move closer to it and copy it again.

3. Copy a masterpiece. As you do so, you will see through the masters' eyes.

4. Note interesting themes and compositions and copy those.

You can also develop them later or simply create internal templates for your own work.

5. You can also search for a gallery piece you ordinarily would not be attracted to and copy it in your sketchbook.

6. If the museum you visit has sculptures, especially life-size ones, draw them one by one. Notice how the artwork's medium affects its appearance. Take some notes on that.

Sculptures allow viewers to see them from all sides. Take advantage of these views and draw the sculpture you choose from these vantage points.

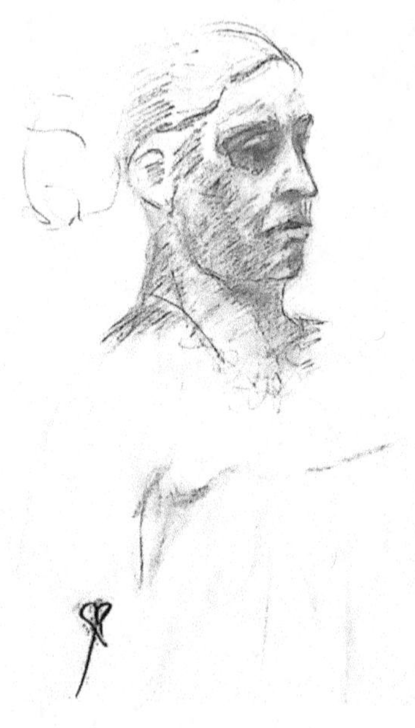

Chapter Thirteen

Drawing the Head and the Face

Rendering Structure and Planes

FACES HOLD SPECIAL SIGNIFICANCE for all human beings. They attract us because they convey emotions and identity. When the underlying head structure is drawn to scale and well, features like eyes, noses, and mouths reflect the subject's essence.

1. Draw several studies of the human skull from various vantage points:

- The side

- The front

- The back

- With an open jaw

- With a closed jaw

2. Draw a male head, then a female head.

3. Use the studies you completed in exercises 1 and 2 and overlay them with tracing paper. Then layer in the muscles of the head.

4. Employ the various vantage points of the skull (see no. 1 above) and compose a drawing in which you put all of them on one page. Better yet, overlap some of these forms in your composition.

Complete several of these drawings, working in different media.

You may also overlay the finished drawing with transparent paper, then draw in the muscles where appropriate.

5. Draw at least 5 to 10 heads in different perspectives: tilted to either one side or another, from above, from below, from the sides, and so on.

6. Go to a public place where you will see many people in quick succession. This could be in a park, at a bus stop, or on a city street.

Draw the gesture of the heads you see in your sketchbook. You'll have to be quick and efficient because none of these models are posing for you. They are simply going about their day and unaware of you.

Incorporate this exercise into your drawing practice routine regularly.

Start with only fifteen (15) minutes of practice and increase the time intervals as you are ready to do so.

You may draw many head gestures on one (1). The paper size will be that of your sketchbook versus a large sheet of paper. But, although the scale is different, the gestures of the head and features capture attitude and character of the people you are drawing.

These gesture drawings are quick studies of sometimes only 10 or 15 seconds.

7. Set up your easel or chair in front of a mirror. Now you are the subject of your drawing. Make sure you have a spotlight to light yourself. Try out different angles and poses.

Here comes your first self portrait. Draw the entire head and its planes first.

Ensure its connection to the neck and even the shoulders. Don't let the head float!

8. Regularly draw your own portrait. You can use props such as hats, feathers, masks, scarves etc. to make the compositions interesting.

9. Another self portrait; this time work on suggestion motion. A quick reminder is that all motion suggested in drawing anything, including the head, arises from capturing and revisiting the gesture.

10. Go to a museum and locate portraits on exhibit there. Contemplate them in terms of perspective, light and shade, anatomy, negative space, composition, and expression. Take notes on what you observe.

Next, copy that drawing into your sketchbook. I do not recommend taking a picture as you are likely to miss important details working from a photograph.

If you love portraiture, make this a weekly practice. Focus on one portrait that appeals to you every week.

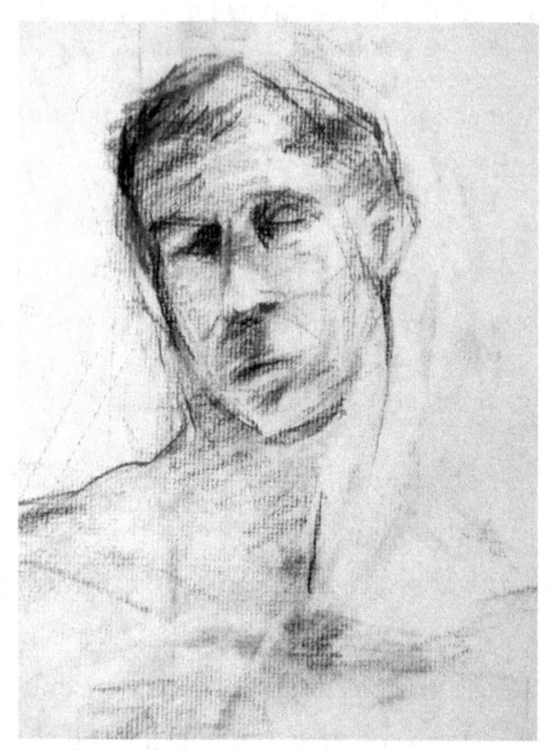

Chapter Fourteen

Head and Face Continued

Drawing Head, Face and Features

Now let's move on to the features.

1. Complete a line drawing of your face.

2. Draw a baby's head either from a model or a photograph.

3. Draw a child's head either from a model or a photograph.

4. Draw a young adult's head either from a model or a photograph.

5. Draw a middle age adult's head either from a model or a photograph.

6. Draw the head of a senior either from a model or a photograph.

Eyes

1. Draw the dark eyes of a woman

2. Draw the light eyes of a woman

3. Draw the eyes of a baby

4. Draw the eyes of a child

5. Draw the eyes of a senior

6. Draw the light eyes of a man

7. Draw the dark eyes of a man

Either use a model or a photograph. You can add to these exercises by repeating them by drawing these eyes from different angles.

Noses

1. Draw side views of several noses

2. Draw the front view of several noses

3. Draw nose of a baby

4. Draw the nose of a child

5. Draw the nose of an adult

6. Draw a nose viewed from below

7. Draw nose viewed from above

Ears

To begin with, think of the ear as fitting into an oval which attaches to the head at an angle. Measure the angle and cross-reference the place where the ear attaches with the nose to position it right.

Fit the outer and inner rims and the other ear forms mentioned above into the imaginary or lightly rendered angled oval shape. Then begin to shade the forms according to what you see. Ensure enough contrast in your shading.

As with other forms, shading these forms of the ear lends them depth and three-dimensionality.

Just as with eyes and noses, ears look different from different angles and viewpoints, so practice them just as you did eyes and noses.

1. Find 10 photographs of faces and copy only the ears.
You may put all of them on one sheet of paper.

Mouths

Mouths curve onto a portion of the face. For our purposes, let's consider the head/face a cylindrical shape. The outer points of the lips, their corners can be cross-referenced with the pupils of the eyes when viewed from the front. I give you these reference points because they help relate the facial features and forms. As always, use your measuring stick to help you with alignment and angles.

Even though mouths are quite expressive because they move when talking, chewing, laughing, crying, and so on, capturing these emotions and their expressions is far from easy. Many emotions are fleeting and in constant flux.

Shading is imperative, as it is with all features. As for teeth, draw them abstractly and match them to the person's whites of the eye. Teeth rarely are a brilliant white color. They also look strange at best when outlined, so stick to the shading.

1. Find 10 photographs of faces. Copy only the mouths.
You may put all of them on one sheet of paper.

2. Draw teeth by shading them.
Do not use lines for them.

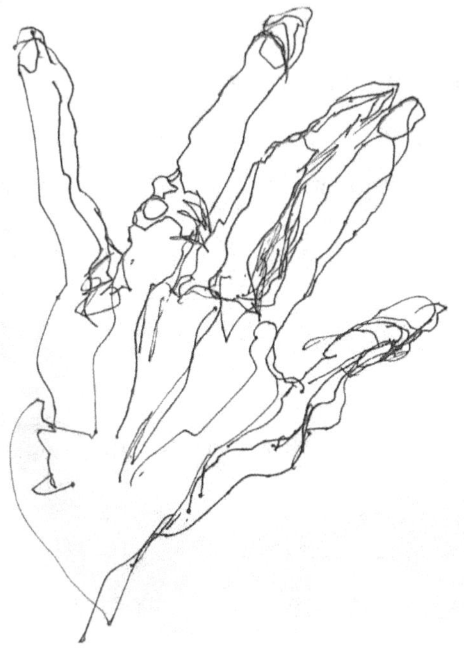

Chapter Fifteen

Drawing Hands

LIKE THE FACE, HANDS are expressive and convey much about the person to whom they belong. This applies to hands all by themselves and to any adornments on them.—Hands do not exist in a vacuum. They connect to the rest of the body through the wrists and arms. Keep this in mind when drawing them.

1. Abstract the hand by drawing its planes.

2. Shade the planes, sticking to two values.

3. Undertake a contour drawing of the hand: yours or your model's.

4. Draw the anatomy of the hand.

5. Draw hands in various positions onto one page.

6. Draw your right and left hand.
Unless you are ambidextrous, you have a dominant hand. For this drawing, you will also use your non-dominant hand.

7. Draw hands in various positions onto one page, this time overlapping them.

8. Abstract the hand into its geometrical forms.

9. Draw hands in a prayer position.

10. Draw hands in a palm up position.

11. Draw hands in a palm down position.

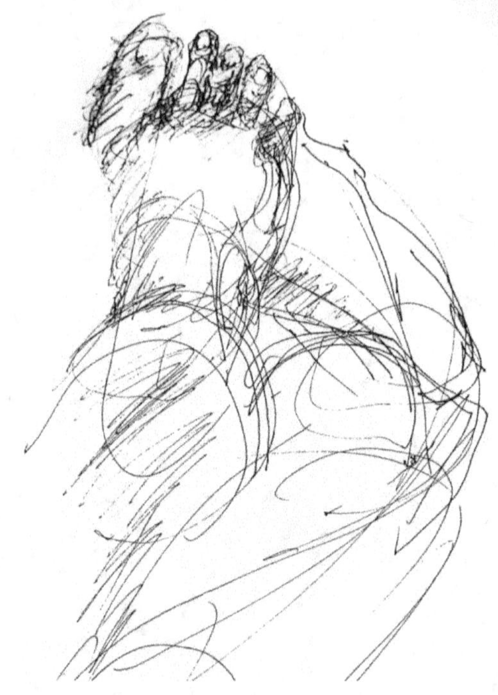

Chapter Sixteen

Drawing Feet

JUST LIKE HANDS, FEET relay information about the person to whom they belong. They carry the weight of the body and stand on the ground. They have personality and so do the shoes that clad them. Connect the feet to the ankles and even to the legs. Also give them a ground.

1. Abstract the foot by drawing its planes.

2. Shade the planes, sticking to two values.

3. Undertake a contour drawing of the foot: yours or your model's.

4. Draw the anatomy of the foot.

5. Draw feet in various positions onto one page.

6. Draw your right and left foot.

7. Draw feet in various positions onto one page, this time overlapping them.

8. Abstract the foot into its geometrical forms.

9. Draw a foot with curled toes.

10. Draw feet from above.

11. Draw feet from below.

12. Draw feet from the side.

13. Draw the feet as shoes cover them.

14. Complete a study of feet bearing the weight of the body

- From the front

- From the side

- From the back

- When standing on tippy toes.

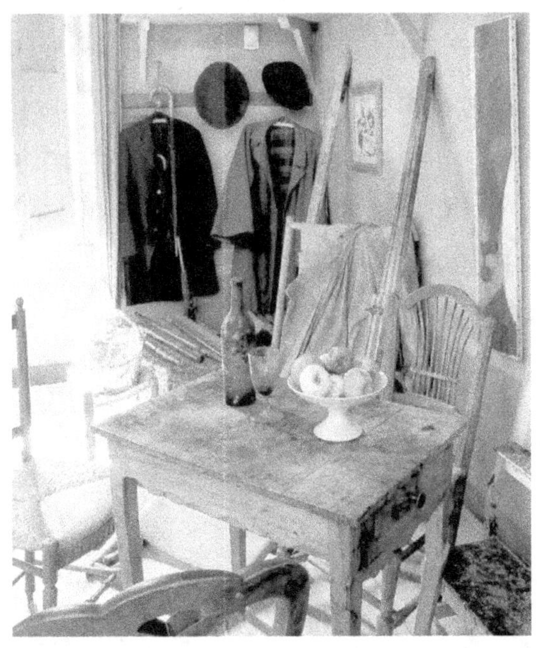

Chapter Seventeen

Settings

Assessing Your Drawing Environment

AFTER CONTEMPLATING FOR A long while whether to include this short section on drawing settings and materials, I now believe it vital to do so. Consider it a brief introduction to figure drawing settings and materials you may employ.

It is hardly comprehensive and intended to invite the artists reading this book to experiment and investigate further. I am only providing a few choice items for artists to consider. Find a good book or two or three about art materials. The appendix mentions several.

Few books mention the setting where you draw and how you set up your workspace. I believe that is too bad because just the setup and drawing environment often make a tremendous difference.

While I recommend you read this section and devote some thought to it, you naturally can easily skip it to forward to the exercise sections.

> There are three important factors in all human activity: spirit, materials, and action.
>
> Chiang Kai-shek

The stage or platform

If you are lucky enough to have a live model, either in a class setting or a private setting, the model must be on a platform so you can view the entire figure without losing it. If you take an online class, those that sprang up all over during the pandemic, find a class with a facilitator or instructor who knows this important piece of posing a model. The facilitator's camera must be able to accommodate the platform, different angles and perspectives of it, and so on.

Lighting

The above also applies to lighting. Lighting is an art all on its own. It can help or hinder your drawing. Use a spotlight on the model, not a flood light. Too much back light washes out the model and her pose. Correct lighting stresses certain parts of a pose and of the model.

When lighting the human figure, the model, these are the options:

- Lighting from above creates a fairly even distribution of shadows and highlights.

- Lighting from the front flattens.

- Lighting from the left throws the right side of the figure into shadow.

- Lighting from the right throws the left side of the figure into shadow.

- Lighting from behind emphasizes the silhouette. It lends ambiguity.

The Model

The model brings a live, three-dimensional body that has attitude, beauty, and idiosyncrasies.

The flesh of the body moves differently on skinny or fat people. Skinny models allow artists to see parts of the skeleton underlying the body. On hefty models, that is much harder and sometimes impossible to see. In either case, the study of anatomy and of the muscles in your spare time affords you the understanding needed to draw either body type. Note also that drawing a skinny model can be quite challenging.

Tautness, muscularity, underlying structure, weight, weightiness, and weight distribution all inform what you see. How flesh moves comprises an inner and an outer component, both of which lend attitude.

An instructor who knows how to direct a model is valuable, and yes, the model earns his or her stipend with such an instructor. A great instructor directs a model to pose according to whatever specific teaching aims. These may include foreshortening, light and shadow work, work on specific body parts, long poses, short poses, and the list goes on.

An outstanding model is trained in all these aspects and one responsive to the instructor's work requests. Many such models understand movement well. They may be dancers or athletes in their regular work. As an aside, urban areas often have a model's guild offering professional models.

Modeling is hard work because it takes immense focus and the ability to adapt to instructor directions and to various environments. Modeling also happens in intimate environments and therefore is quite personal. Students owe the model respect and gratitude.

Sometimes professional models are not available for various reasons. In those cases, students may take turns modeling for each other, fully dressed.

Standing or sitting to draw

Both standing at an easel or sitting on a drawing horse work well. However, there are distinct differences that affect the drawing because of the perspective involved when sitting or standing. In either case, make sure you are close to the model, your materials are ready, your body is relaxed, and distractions are gone, or at a minimum. No cell phones, no chatting with classmates and the like.

Some instructors play music. That is fine so long as the music is soothing and does not distract from drawing the figure. Distracting music could be the genre that is playing or the volume at which it plays. If you find the music played affects you in an adverse way, mention this to the instructor.

Easels

Standing easels or drawing horses usually are available in classrooms and art studios. Which one you choose and where either is located in the room and in proximity to the model makes a difference to your drawing session. That is because easels and drawing horses offer different drawing perspectives to you.

When sitting on a drawing horse, your vantage point is generally somewhere below the model's head. Standing at an easel usually puts you on a level with the model almost seeing face to face.

I like working at an easel to draw because standing at an easel provides me the perspective I most appreciate. It also demands my full attention when drawing. Perhaps even more importantly, standing at an easel and drawing requires my own body to coordinate and to feel the pose of the model.

Of course, you can also sit on a drawing stool, but your perspective and body coordination will be different. Experiment and find out what works for you.

One final word on standing at an easel regards consideration for fellow artists in the room. Awareness of others is important so as not to obstruct their view of the model. Unless no one sits on the drawing horse in front of which you wish to set up your easel, move to another space in the room.

Arrive early to set up your workspace to your liking, keeping others in mind. It is often advantageous to walk around the room first to assess what might work best for you for the drawing session. Seeing the model often also helps you make a good decision about your set-up.

To chat or to focus

You might find yourself in an environment which may work or not work for you, depending on the art class you attend.

I find that a *process* happens inside me when entering drawing mode. It happens inside me when I draw, and that process simultaneously translates to the paper. It's a mindset, a kind of internal set-up that lasts throughout the drawing session.

The model in front of me represents a physical presence that demands full attention. I often see slight movements in the model's skin that reinforce the living quality that I seek to translate, the many movements, seen and unseen, that happen in the body at all times.

What I observe and see is the overall gesture, but it is fed by innumerable other gestures which can only be intuited rather than fully *seen*. Intuition, of course, is a kind of seeing, and it demands meticulous application. It is internal and chatting distracts from it or even eliminates it.

Equally important is that everything in front of me must go through my body first, through my perceptive organs. I must feel the pose in front of me as though I were to inhabit it myself. This demands proprioception and the stillness of mind that sometimes goes by the name of contemplation.

All seeing is transformation. It is the alchemy of the processes of life. But how all this gets framed or composed makes a vast difference in what translates, what others relate to and see. This requires immense focus and trust, something that may take many drawings to achieve. Hundreds of mediocre drawings often precede one great one.

What does all this have to do with the environment you find yourself in class, in a drawing group, or elsewhere?

The drawing environment sets the tone. When draughtsmen and -women chat, pay attention to their phones etc., their concentration and focus suffer. This can also happen with some music choices. Many teachers understand this, and some artists do while others don't. Wisely choose your environment for drawing and aim to respect fellow artists if drawing in a group.

As an aside, during the pandemic I signed up for an online figure drawing class in which the music was so distracting and dissonant that I had to turn on silent mode. If you must listen to your own choice of music, bring along earbuds. Just realize that even with earbuds others still may hear your music or at least the drone of it.

On-line Drawing Sessions

The pandemic isolated many of us from events, classes and outings we were used to. Many events and get-togethers went virtual. While it was wonderful to have models appear on my computer screen, a few drawbacks reared their ugly heads.

One of them was sessions put on by unqualified facilitators who knew little or nothing about how to set up the space, the model, the camera, the entire session. Most were private individuals versus actual art instructors.

Online figure drawing sessions also attracted men and women who had never modeled before then and knew nothing about modeling. Perhaps it was just an easy way to make a few extra dollars from home. Many times these models posed in bizarre ways, feet cut off and all the rest. Just because someone will undress does not mean they are worthwhile models.

Yet another drawback is that your computer screen shows you a model that is nothing close to life size. The screen reduces detail and frames the figure in a way that is unnatural.

Be aware of these possible drawbacks and know that they affect how you draw and especially whether you will be fully engaged in the activity. Even though you may be in a drawing class, the artistic endeavor of drawing is quite solitary. You are sharing space with others who want to engage their vision and improve their skills. The respect I mentioned in regard to the model equally applies to your fellow students and artists.

One more caveat that applies to models, whether in an in person art class or online: no photography of the model is allowed for privacy and other reasons.

Naturally, this is much harder to enforce when the class is online and some online classes allow their participants to snap photos for additional pay. Do the honorable and refrain from taking pictures of the model.

Nevertheless, there is value in online figure drawing sessions. They are accessible, low cost, and convenient. As long as you are aware of the pros and cons of them, they provide you with practice sessions you might otherwise lack.

Now let's move on to selecting the art materials that work for you.

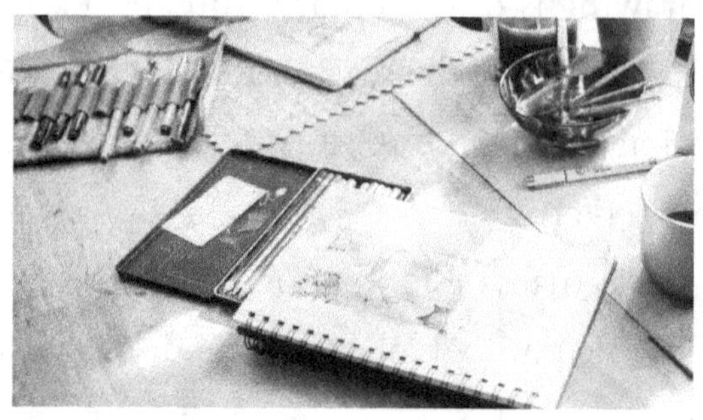

Chapter Eighteen

Materials

Deciding with What to Draw

ARTISTS EMPLOY A SMORGASBORD of materials. It's fun to pick them, experiment with them, and find those that appeal most. This section offers some suggestions about where to start and what to look for.

Paper

Drawing papers are as personal as the media you use to draw. Whether your drawing medium is pen and ink, watercolor, pencil, or charcoal affects your choice of paper because each medium has particular qualities and peculiarities.

All papers come in various sizes. Some have varied tooth. Tooth refers to the surface of the paper, whether it is smooth or rough. All produce different effects and affect how your pencil, charcoal, ink, or watercolor interact and reflect.

The standard art class paper format is 18x24. If you opt for it, use newsprint and higher quality drawing papers. Note that newsprint is a cheap paper that yellows and degrades. Your newsprint drawing follows suit.

Archival quality papers, which are acid free, are more expensive but certainly worth the expense.

Experiment with different formats and materials to find what works best for you.

Note that all materials you use for drawing have a connection to what the eye sees and are tactile as well. Here are some options for you to explore:

Experiment with various papers from different manufacturers to find the best ones for you, always considering the drawing medium you prefer.

Newsprint

- A cheap, thin, rougher non-archival paper.
- Will yellow and degrade over time.
- Great for warm-up sketches.

Paper Vellum

- Either made from tree bark fibers or rag cotton
- A translucent, lower priced paper.

- Often used for blueprints and architectural drawings.
- Sensitive to humidity.
- It is suitable for use as a drawing paper; best for pencil work.
- Waterproof velum exists.
- It is less absorbent than watercolor paper.

Watercolor paper

- Comes in many varieties and sizes.
- High absorption watercolor paper is pure cotton.
- Pure cotton watercolor paper is expensive.
- Cellulose or wood pulp watercolor paper is a cheaper alternative.
- Has different weights and sizes.
- The best weight is 140 lbs or more.
- The smaller the size, the more difficult to handle and control.
- Three types of watercolor paper exist. Each has different surface qualities.
  o Cold-press has some texture.
  o Hot press is smooth.
  o Rough press has a rough, textured surface.
- Available in rolls.

Charcoal paper

- Paper titled charcoal paper usually has a tooth to it.
- Smooth papers do not work well with charcoal.
- Comes in different sizes and weights.
- Weights usually range between 60 and 90 lbs.

- Look for archival quality paper.
- Available in rolls.
- Comes in various colors.
- Can be smooth for detail work with charcoal pencils
- Or textured for working with charcoal sticks.
- Always have a kneaded eraser at the ready.
- Charcoal is malleable and moves around.
- Try fixative to keep your drawing in place on the paper.

o Caution: fixative takes special application and can help or hinder your work.

Mylar

- Is a paper coated with polyester on one or both sides.
- Is translucent and strong.
- Allows for erasing.
- Does not yellow.
- Lasts a long time.
- Best with pen and ink, markers, graphite and colored pencils.
- May be expensive.

Note: mylar sleeves often serve to protect artwork. They are not the same as mylar paper.

Sketchbooks

Sketchbooks are indispensable to any artist. They come in many varieties and sizes. Find one or two that works for you and easy to take along wherever you go. You may find, as I did, that certain sizes are too large and cumbersome to carry around with you.

Your sketchbook, large or small, alongside a pencil or pen, offers the opportunity to draw almost anywhere. That could be in a park, a museum, a café, at home, or many other places. I enjoy the ballet and the symphony and take my sketchbook when going there. The low light in these venues forces me to draw quick gestural sketches while trusting my drawing ability. I also often draw from memory after the performance.

I mention this to give you more ideas about using sketchbooks. They are such great tools for anyone who loves drawing and aims to develop drawing skills. This applies to drawing any object, but it is particularly compelling when drawing the figure.

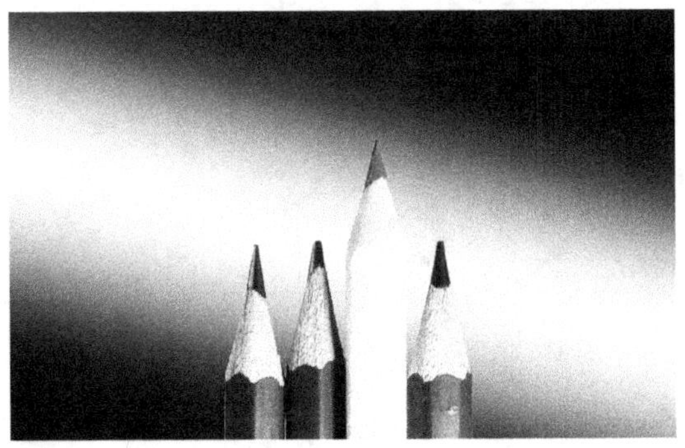

Chapter Nineteen

Drawing media

Choosing Your Medium

As with materials, the choice of drawing media is considerable. And there often are new variations on materials. Spending an afternoon in an art store to play a little is just plain fun. In the meantime, here are some with which to begin that journey.

Drawing media include

Charcoal—soft, medium, hard

- Available in stick and pencil form

- The softer the charcoal, the deeper its tone.

Pen and ink

- Allows for easy work in various techniques, such as hatching and cross-hatching, scribbling and dotting and others.

- Easy to use on almost any paper.

- Ink pen choices are many. Look for a pen with an ink flow that you like. Test them out at the art store of your choice.

- Ink is available in various colors.

- You can also buy an ink well and a quill.

- Lends itself to drawing details.

- Great for quick sketches.

- Creates permanent drawings. That is both a pro and a con.

- Although erasable ink is available, experiment with it first.

- Low cost.

Chalk

- Differs from pastels.

- Masters like Leonardo DaVinci (1452-1519) often used

white and red chalk in drawings.

- Versatile uses.

- Comes in different varieties.

- Easy to blend and layer.

- Cheap

- Easy cleanup.

Watercolors

- Are water-soluble paints.

- Always respond to water, including when dry.

- Create washes of subtle beauty.

- Are available in watercolor palettes, tubes, and watercolor pencils.

- Are great for accenting drawings in other media, such as pencils.

- Lend themselves to various techniques.

- Are wonderful for studying values.

- Watercolor paints and pads can be pricey.

Pencils, including graphite, oil-based, and colored pencils

- Pencil lead varies in hardness and blackness.

Know that although the word "lead" appears here, pencils do not contain lead. Instead, they most often contain a mixture of graphite and clay. Pencils with mostly graphite are known as graphite pencils.

- "B" refers to the blackness (HB, B, 2B, 3B, 4B, 5B, 6B, 7B, 8B, 9B)

- "H" refers to the hardness of the lead (F, H, 2H, 3H, 4H, 5H, 6H, 7H, 9H)

- The numbers in front refer to the level of blackness or hardness.

- Example: 5H would be the hardest lead and lightest color, and 8B represents the darkest black.

- Graphite pencils, composed almost entirely of graphite, create rich, dark marks.

- Oil-based colored pencils contain rich pigments, are great for adding layers and shades, and are difficult to erase.

- Watercolor pencils are wonderful for drawing and shading. They have a watercolor effect when using a wet brush on them.

- Colored pencils are for drawing and shading. They do not respond to water.

Crayons and crayon pencils

- Contain wax, pigment and clay.

- Use them for drawing and shading.

- Their colors are rich.

- Although some erasable crayon pencils exist, it is impossible to erase crayon drawing marks in their entirety.

Gouache

- Richly pigmented water-based paint.

- It dries faster than watercolor.

- Has a matte, flat finish.

- Can be expensive. Pricing depends on pigment content.

- It is opaque (as opposed to watercolor).

- Beginner friendly.

Pastels

- Many types of pastels exist: chalk pastels (not the same as chalk!), oil pastels, pastel pencils, hard and soft pastels, and so on.

- All types require different techniques and applications.

- Experiment and take a class to learn more about them.

- Allow for layered work.

- Rich colors.

- Easy to blend.

- Can be expensive.

Oils

- Usually made of linseed oil and pigment.

- They have a strong odor and require solvents like turpentine.

  - The solvents are toxic.

- Have a timeless feel to them.

- Can get muddy, depending on application.

- Take time to dry.

- Add depth and texture, especially when applied in layers.

- Great for those interested in painting and in exploring color.

- Canvases need prepping when painting with oil.

- Costly paints.

- Have a yellow tone to them when dry.

Acrylics

- Water-based paints.

- You have the option to apply it thickly to the canvas or in a more translucent fashion.

- Quick drying.

- Offer vibrant colors.

- Applicable to a variety of surfaces, such as paper, canvas, and others.

These are the most common ones for drawing, though I have included some options that progress to painting. All media have different qualities and uses.

Different application techniques also apply to them. Make it your mission to learn how to use each of them. Many good books on art materials and techniques for them exist. See the appendix for some recommendations.

This section gives you a selection of drawing media options. I have included some that move into painting territory because many paintings require drawings first.

Even though several media require brushes, a discussion about them is beyond the scope of this book. Any good book on art materials provides the necessary details on watercolor, acrylic, oil and other brushes.

A quick note: if you love charcoal like I do, have a couple of kneaded erasers handy. They work great to graduate shadows and put in subtle reflected light shades. Using them instead of white highlights will give your drawings a natural look.

Start using materials like pencil, pen and ink and charcoal instead of colors and paints. The reason is that the study of color is a lifelong endeavor and that color can easily mislead and distract from your drawing.

Media that offer color options to you, while exciting, also have drawbacks. The study of color comprises a gargantuan field. Color choices can make or break a drawing because colors must work together in effective and visually decipherable ways. Some colors recede while others project forward. All colors have psychological properties which affect how the drawing reads and evokes varying viewer responses. Until the mastery of other drawing fundamentals, use color sparingly, if at all.

Whether using color, start your drawings lightly so that they stay flexible as you build the drawing. This approach also allows you to layer drawings, thereby providing rich tapestries for them, and to make any corrections with more ease.

Again, experiment with materials until you find those right for you. Gradually add more if that is your desire.

Other Considerations

When putting together your art supplies shopping list, plan to get the best art supplies you can afford.

You may also wish to set up a drawing space or even a studio in your home. Set it up so you feel comfortable and peaceful in the space and your art supplies are at the ready.

In case you like to draw outside, go to museums or travel, put together the art supplies you need. They may differ from what you use in your home or in a classroom. For example, paper sizes that are larger than 9x12 get unwieldy and add the onus of carrying them with you wherever you go.

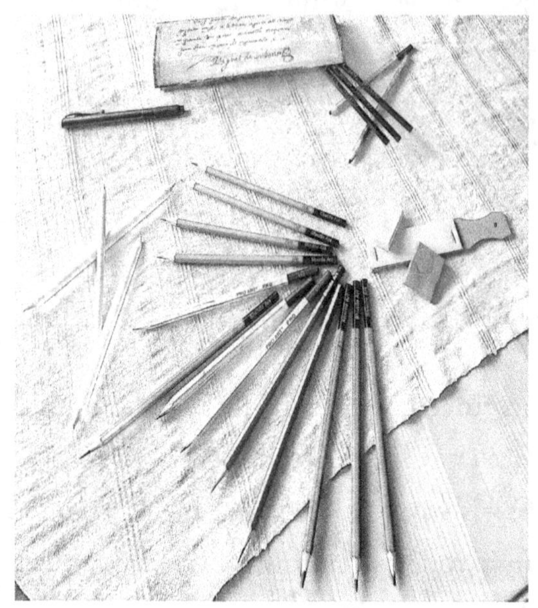

Chapter Twenty

Miscellaneous Drawing Aids

Assisting Your Drawing Efforts

Now that you have more information about paper choices and drawing media, it may delight you to know about other available drawing aids. Add them to your toolbox to move your drawing skills to a new level.

They are simple but powerful and they appear in no particular order below:

Viewfinder

As mentioned in the book which this *Workbook* accompanies, your drawing starts before you ever touch the paper with your drawing tool. You must know what you want to capture. This may sound simple, yet takes mental acuity and preparation.

The model in front of you offers many drawing angles, views and possibilities. You decide how you want to draw the model and whether you want to emphasize a certain aspect of the pose. Visualize this by thinking about how you take a photograph. Shooting pictures blindly, willy-nilly is an unlikely approach.

Instead, your camera's viewfinder helps you to compose the picture you take.

Using a viewfinder, mostly self-made, is a great way to do the same when beginning a drawing.

Make a viewfinder from a piece of cardboard and use it to see the model and her pose in a new way. It helps you arrange your composition. You may also use it to crop certain things.

But it is so much more than just a compositional tool because it allows you to see the model and the pose in space through a frame. That frame is movable because you hold it in your hand and look through the frames opening.

Okay, now let's make the view finder, unless you want to buy it in an art store for a pretty penny. Take a piece of cardboard that is square or rectangular. You determine the size. Just remember it ought to be easy to hold and therefore fairly small. Mine is 8.5x10, a rectangle with cut out in the middle of 2x3 in it. It works for me.

Use your new viewfinder like this:

Either hold the viewfinder at arm's length or close to your eye. I find it easiest to close one eye when looking through it at the model or the scene in front of me. Find what works for you to establish the focus of your composition.

Now that you have taken in how your composition will work, look at your paper to envision how what you just decided will work and fit on your paper. My method is to draw a border in the paper in order to keep the composition on the paper. Many artists have a different approach, one that is borderless. In that case, the paper size itself dictates the borders.

Perhaps you need to look through the viewfinder one or more times mentally to translate your vision to the paper in front of you. That's fine. Once you complete this part of starting a drawing, put the viewfinder down and pick up your sighting stick, if you have not already done so.

Using a viewfinder takes a little getting used to, but you will be a pro in short order.

Sighting stick

Sighting sticks are such great tools when drawing anything. I use a wooden BBQ skewer or a sharpened pencil, and hold it in my dominant hand with the thumb indicating the measure I establish when looking at the model or the object in front of me.

Before detailing how to sight the model or object you wish to draw, it is important to understand the functions the sighting stick fulfills. Whatever you draw exists in an ambient setting, not in a vacuum. The setting and the model or object stand in relationship to one another. This is also true for the many elements that make up the model or object, the contours and the internal structural elements.

A sighting stick will help you see the model you draw in a new light and relate him or her to the environment: a chair, a platform, a wall, a room, and so forth. That is valuable for great compositions and in fitting your subject onto the page.

The stick does this via you holding it to compare the angles present. For example, if the model sits in a chair and leans back, the elements closer to you come forward while others recede in space. Yes, this is called foreshortening, and it means some shapes are hidden from your view and some appear shorter, visually speaking. To understand this better, use your sighting stick to assess which angles relate to which others.

A good point of reference for this is the pit of the throat. When the model takes the reclining pose just described, the hips, legs and feet are likely to come forward, at least one of them. Clearly, this depends on the exact pose.

For our general discussion here, the sighting stick gives you the angles at which the head sits on the neck and shoulders, where the body's weight lives in the pose, how the torso lengthens or shortens, and how the arms and legs project from the torso. These are examples only because there are many more angles to behold in the body and its environment.

All angles and their measurements relate to one another and enable you to compare and analyze the forms in front of you. Consider them scaffolding, though they may also be gestural. Your sighting stick provides you the ability to construct the pose correctly so that the viewer immediately understands what she is looking at.

You are checking the angles of lines against both vertical and horizontal lines of the sighting stick. Hold your stick at arm's length and keep the stick straight versus tilting it. Use it vertically or horizontally and you will read the angles with ease, so long as the stick is straight.

The measure unit you use on the sighting stick derives from holding it between your thumb and index finger with the thumb marking the vertical size of the head, then comparing this measurement to the other body elements you are drawing. You will comprehend the angles, the comparative measurements, and how poses recede or project into space.

As with anything, using the sighting stick takes a little getting used to, but your drawings immeasurably benefit from this simple tool.

Kneaded eraser

Kneaded erasers are indispensable to you because you can shape them to fine points. This means you can erase fine details an ordinary eraser fails to get.

That's also because of the pliable quality of the kneaded eraser versus the hardness of regular erasers.

Kneaded erasers therefore are easy on the underlying paper, while regular erasers can chafe through the paper and leave obvious unintended marks.

Consider the kneaded eraser a drawing tool, one that is preferable to lift out and emphasize highlights. In many cases, it takes the place of white chalk.

As you use a kneaded eraser, it will pick up plenty of the drawing medium, especially in the case of pastels and charcoal. Keep kneaded erasers in a plastic bag so they stay cleaner longer. Some artists claim that you can wash kneaded erasers. I have had mediocre to dismal success with that. By all means, test it out, but have several kneaded erasers handy in any case.

Paper Stomps

Paper stomps or stumps are especially helpful when drawing with pencil or charcoal. You can blend or smudge with them and render softer, more natural appearing lines. They come in various sizes and varieties. I use the soft stomps for my charcoal work. You, of course, may find other varieties better suited to the work you do.

Once used, you can easily clean their tips with sandpaper.

You could also use a tortillon, which is a stomp made of rolled paper. The rolled paper might leave ridges, which are often difficult to remove, on your drawing. Proceed with caution if you choose to use them.

Sandpaper

Sandpaper is quite useful when pencil sharpeners will use up your valuable drawing media. Charcoal pencils are a case in point. When using pencil sharpeners, charcoal pencils often break off, leaving you to keep sharpening for more of the same. Sandpaper works much better. And as already mentioned, use them to clean paper stomps.

Pencil sharpener

Pencil sharpeners still belong in your toolbox. Use them for pencils and colored pencils. They work.

Some pencil sharpeners are better than others. Some artists swear by electric pencil sharpeners, but much depends on the type of pencil you want to sharpen. Pencils with softer materials in them or charcoal pencils can be harder to sharpen.

A razor blade comes in mighty handy when sharpening charcoal pencils because you have more control over the sharpening angle and can see how best to sharpen these pencils without wasting the interior charcoal in them.

Clean the sharpeners as soon as you use them so they are ready for the next go-around and the shavings end up in the trash, not in your toolbox or on the floor.

Drawing board

Drawing and sketching boards come in varieties, some with clips to hold your paper or pad. They also come in various sizes and provide a flat, stable, and sturdy surface. That is invaluable for correct measurements with your sighting stick.

Their clips stabilize the paper or paper pad, though I recommend having a couple more clips on hand in case you change paper direction from portrait to landscape layout.

In case of a sheet of drawing paper, you might explore taping the paper onto the board with masking tape. If you find the board provided too hard a surface for your drawing purposes, experiment with a few additional sheets below your sheet. However, taping the paper to the board may now work in that case.

You also get ergonomic benefits when using a drawing board. No more bending over or slouching!

Drawing boards work even better in combination with a standing easel.

Chamois

Chamois is a cloth made of animal skin, usually sheep skin. It is soft and pliable and works well for blending, smoothing, lightening, and even adding texture to dry media drawings. All you need is a small piece of chamois, but consider having several pieces at the ready.

Art stores sell chamois in small sizes. They charge a premium for them. Automotive stores carry them, generally under the name of "leather cloth." There they come in large sizes and are a good amount cheaper than the art store ones. I purchase them at automotive stores and cut them to my preferred size.

Once purchased, wash them in lukewarm water before use, then hang them to dry. Wash them by hand versus in a washing machine.

Dry them naturally and stay away from letting them dry in the sun or near a heater in your home as the chamois will become stiff and lose its soft qualities.

After you use the chamois when creating art, rinse it in warm and soapy water, using natural soap only. Use soap sparingly, so no soap residues remain when done. Hang the chamois to dry as described in the previous paragraph.

Taking care of your chamois this way ensures a long life for it and keeps it soft and absorbent. Store it only once is completely dry because the leather cloth easily can mold and rot when left wet or damp.

In case your chamois becomes dry or stiff after washing it and drying it, first rub it against a hard surface to restore its natural qualities. If that fails to work, the chamois may need a little oil mixed with water to restore it. Soak it in this mixture for no longer than ten minutes. Hopefully, that does the trick.

Clean up

Creating art often is a messy endeavor. While that is part of the fun, cleaning up afterwards is part of working as an artist. Yes, it's less exciting than creating art, yet it helps elevate your productivity. After all, it's great to know where all your materials are and that they are ready for your next art session.

The same applies to the space where you create your drawings. Different media present different cleanup challenges. For example, drawing with charcoal is dusty, and charcoal particles settle on the easel and the surrounding floor. It also covers your drawing hand in dust, so be careful touching anything, including the edges of your drawing.

To clean up after a charcoal drawing session, close your drawing pad and stand it against the drawing board or better yet lay it flat onto a safe surface. Put away your art materials in the bin or box you use. Use a paper towel to wipe down the easel and assess whether any of your charcoal stick are on the floor and retrieve them.

Some class settings and studios do the floor cleanup for you, but to help them maintain great art spaces perhaps bring a drop cloth to place under the easel. In your home space or studio, a drop cloth saves you from tracking charcoal dust all over the home or apartment. And regular vacuuming helps.

These tips apply to pastels as well because they are just as dusty as charcoal.

Charcoal draws moisture out of your skin and sometimes is hard to get off your hands and the fingernails affected by it. Wash your hands to the best of your ability and use a fingernail brush. Restore the moisture in your hands with a good hand cream, one with enough fat content to do so without leaving your hands greasy.

For those of you working with watercolors, clean your watercolor cakes and palette and brushes right away when finishing your art session. Rinsing them under running water is often sufficient. You can also use a small sponge to remove any residues on your palette.

The watercolor cakes will dry out and crack over time. Storing them in a box away from air prevents that from happening and keeps them in good condition for a long time. If you use watercolor tubes, tighten their caps well. That way they will keep a long time as well.

After rinsing watercolor brushes with water, gently flick the brushes by snapping your wrist to remove excess water. Then lay the brushes with the brush head slanted downward to dry on either a paper towel or other absorbent towel. Putting the brushes upright eventually destroys it. It allows any remaining water into the metal cap that holds the bristles. We also call this cap the ferrule.

When water drains into the ferrule, it eventually causes the brush to lose its shape and function because the wood handle swells and the brush bristles spread. Fine strokes become impossible when that happens. Therefore, good brush care becomes indispensable.

The same happens when immersing the brush into a full cup of water. Only the bristles should be in water when drawing and painting. Keep the metal cap dry.

Wash your hands with soap and water if any paint is on them. That's it for watercolor cleanup, though also take care that your watercolor work is dry.

Cleaning up after a session with acrylic paints is quite similar to the watercolor clean up. The brush care is the same. However, acrylics dry much faster; to remove dry acrylics off surfaces use rubbing alcohol. Rubbing alcohol is too harsh for use on your hands, however. Remove dried acrylics from your hands with soap□Ivory soap works well. You can also try baby wipes or use a protective cream or lotion, sold at art stores, before your acrylics session.

Note: I am not covering oil paint cleanup because it is more involved, requires solvents, and more substantially veers into the world of painting.

Fixative

Many artists use fixatives to protect works of art. Fixatives are chemical sprays used on dry media. They help to hold or fix volatile drawing media like charcoal and pastels in place. As you draw your piece, the art might smudge because of the dusty nature of these media.

You can use fixative in various ways, including by spraying it on a work in progress to protect what is already on the paper from smudging. Some artists use it before adding color. That way, the pigments stay clean.

Or apply fixative to an already finished part of a drawing. When doing so, that section of the drawing can no longer smudge or suffer rubbing it out.

And you can also spray the fixative on a finished drawing to help protect it from disbursing surface dust from the drawing. Doing so will also protect it from other environmental factors.

Before a quick note on how to apply fixative, please know that there are some drawbacks to using it. Among them are that it can dull your drawings and their colors. Spraying it often requires experimenting with it before using it on a drawing you love.

The best way to apply it is to spray a light coat onto the drawing after having shaken the can. Follow directions on the spray can. These also mention spraying it from a 12 to 18 inch distance in a well-ventilated space. It is a chemical liquid and as such combustible.

You can apply fixative sprays in several layers. You just have to wait until each sprayed layer is dry.

Several types of fixatives exist, so read reviews and speak to knowledgeable art store staff to find the right one for your work.

Portfolios

Get or make a portfolio for your artwork to protect it from the elements. Portfolios save your art and preserve it so that you can either work on the pieces later or mat and frame them later. Portfolios are great and you also organize your drawings that way.

Google the term to find ideas and tutorials for self-made ones. Or go to an art store, either in person or online, and explore the many options.

Dealing with your Paper

Clip your paper pad onto your drawing board. If you have one piece of paper, you may either clip it or tape it onto the board. In case of taping it onto the board, consider whether padding the paper is important to you. Padding can help create a comfortable drawing experience for you, but it is a personal preference. Experiment with it to find out what works best for you.

Use your newsprint pad during the warm-up exercises and short poses. Good paper is expensive and using it after your warm-up exercises often makes the most sense. Switch to good paper, paper with archival qualities and acid-free, for longer poses.

The size and format of your paper supports your compositional efforts. With that in mind, you might find it helpful to either frame or subdivide the paper.

You can do so in the following ways:

A white rectangular frame with black lines

A white rectangular object with a drawn x

Remember that good composition requires knowing what you are after for the drawing you are about to produce. This happens before you ever touch the paper with any medium.

An artist is not paid for his labor but for his vision.

James McNeill Whistler

In figure drawing, always fit the model's pose—yes, the entire figure—on the page. This is especially true for beginners and for staying true to proportions. Once that becomes second nature, the intentional crop becomes much easier and often visually more appealing.

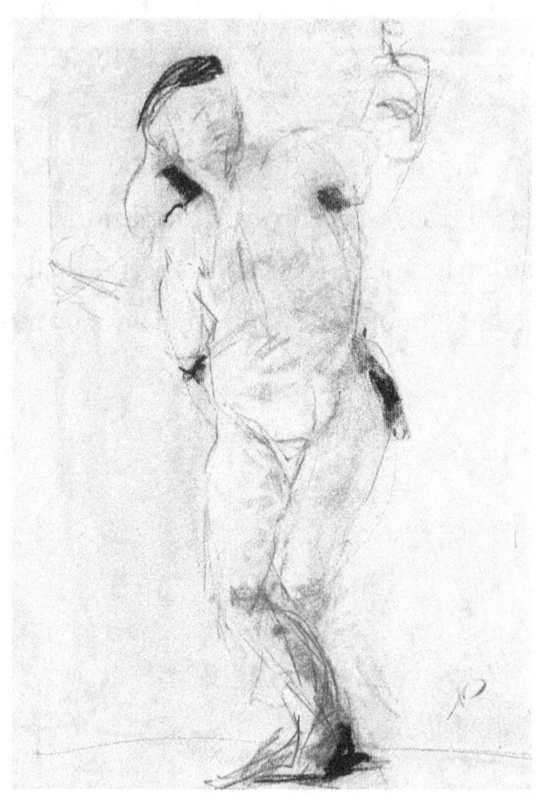

Chapter Twenty-One

Final Remarks

Continuing Your Drawing Practice

THIS SMALL BUT MIGHTY book full of tips and tricks and drawing exercises is hardly all-inclusive. It is meant to ignite your love of drawing and its practice.

The exercises it contains offer endless variations and possibilities.

I restate what I said at the beginning of this exercise section because doing so is that important.

You are on the right track in your quest to become a skilled artist. Only regular, repeated practice brings you closer and closer to that aim. Practice, combined with careful study of the model, the environment, movement, and easy access to several excellent reference books, is tantamount. No other panacea exists.

You can do all exercises in the following sections repeatedly. In fact, that is the only way to master them.

Enjoy the process and every improvement, no matter how small!

It's always too early to quit.

Norman Vincent Peale

And please, let me know how you fare with the exercises, what you like or dislike, and any other figure drawing related comment. You may reach me at info@figuredrawing.life.

And if you found value in these pages and enjoyed them, please leave a review wherever you purchased the book. Perhaps also ask your local library to add this title to its shelves. Thank you!

3% of the proceeds of this book support the arts and artistic expression through inception of a Foundation. Find out more as the Foundation gets up and running.

Appendix

Artist Resources

DRAWING IS A POPULAR subject. This appendix lists just a select few resources to deepen your drawing and figure drawing mastery.

Art Store Websites

https://www.utrechtart.com/
https://www.dickblick.com/
https://www.michaels.com/
https://shop.archsupplies.com/
https://flaxart.com/

Most of these companies are nationwide, or at a minimum ship nationwide.

Many art supply companies sell via Amazon.

Do an online search for re-usable art supplies. Most of these are local. Their aim is to keep art materials out of landfills, since many art materials contain toxic substances. Their prices usually are lower than those of the big chains. You might even score a great art workshop on offer.

Here are two such stores for the San Francisco Bay Area:
https://www.scrap-sf.org/
https://essexlad.com/berkeleycraftsstore/

Books about Art Materials

The Complete Guide to Art Materials and Techniques by Caroline West (Editor)
The Artist's Handbook on Materials and Techniques by Ralph Mayer
The History of Art Materials by A.W.J Pilgrim

Books about Drawing

Complete Book of Drawing: Essential Skills for Every Artist
Anatomy and Drawing by Victor Perard
Figure Drawing Design and Invention by Michael Hampton
Light, Shade and Shadow by E.L. Koller
The Quick Pose: A Compilation of Gestures and Thoughts on Figure Drawing by Erin Meads
Drawing the Head and the Hands by Andrew Loomis
The Power of the Center by Rudolf Arnheim
Art and Visual Perception by Rudolf Arnheim

Also by

Figure Drawing: Rhythm and Language of the Human Form (Vol. I)

The Real Estate Investor Manuals
How Trends Make You A Smarter Investor (Vol. I)
Finding Profitable Deals (Vol. II)
The Art and Science of Real Estate Negotiation (Vol. III)
Investing in Real Estate in YourSelf-Directed IRA (Vol. IV)

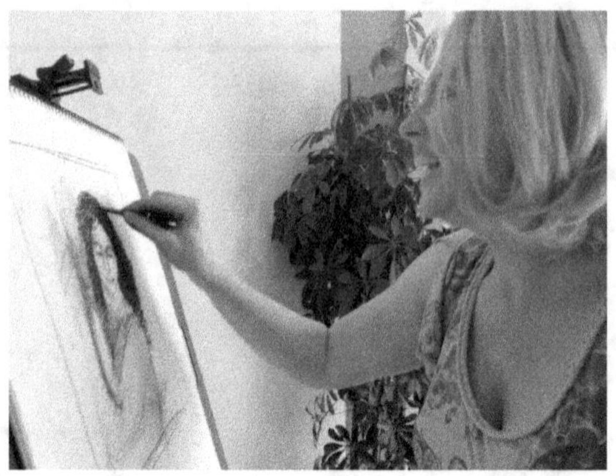

About the author

Gabrielle Dahms is a renaissance woman: artist, author, presenter, and entrepreneur. She holds a master's in history and loves to research and write. Her latest books, *Figure Drawing: Rhythm and Language of the Human Form* and its accompanying *Workbook impart* technical and artistic considerations and knowledge when drawing the human figure. The books cull teachings from over four decades of drawing the figure.□Her other non-fiction publications include the titles in *The Real Estate Investor Manuals* series, and hundreds of articles and blog posts about real estate. When away from the keyboard, she enjoys nature, travel, and other cultures. She also volunteers for local food banks and animal welfare causes.

www.ingramcontent.com/pod-product-compliance
Lightning Source LLC
Chambersburg PA
CBHW070814260726
48660CB00005B/1848